EXPLORING
KNIGHTS
AND
CASTLES

Jonathan Rutland

Designed by David Nash

Illustrators
John Berry · Richard Hook · John Keay
Roger Payne · Charlotte Snook · Bill Stallion

Pan Books · London and Sydney

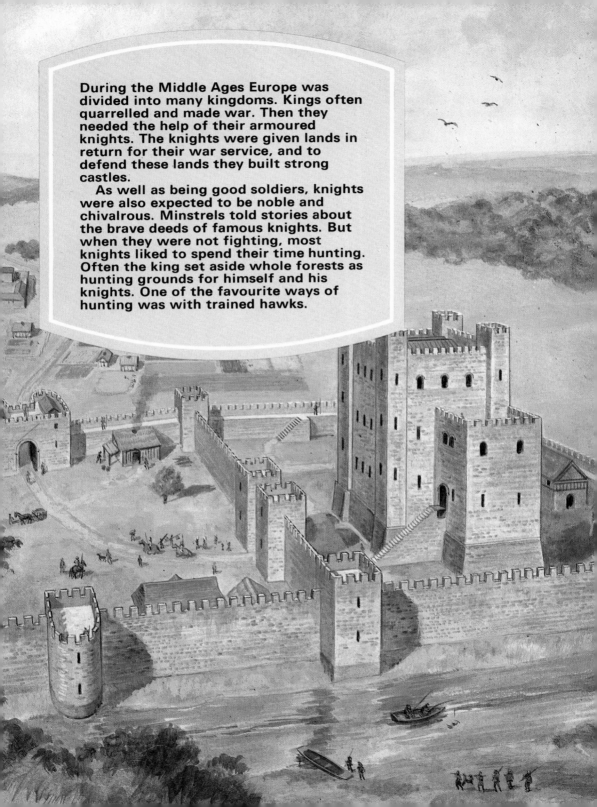

During the Middle Ages Europe was divided into many kingdoms. Kings often quarrelled and made war. Then they needed the help of their armoured knights. The knights were given lands in return for their war service, and to defend these lands they built strong castles.

As well as being good soldiers, knights were also expected to be noble and chivalrous. Minstrels told stories about the brave deeds of famous knights. But when they were not fighting, most knights liked to spend their time hunting. Often the king set aside whole forests as hunting grounds for himself and his knights. One of the favourite ways of hunting was with trained hawks.

lord's chamber

chapel

guardroom

Great Hall

well

storeroom

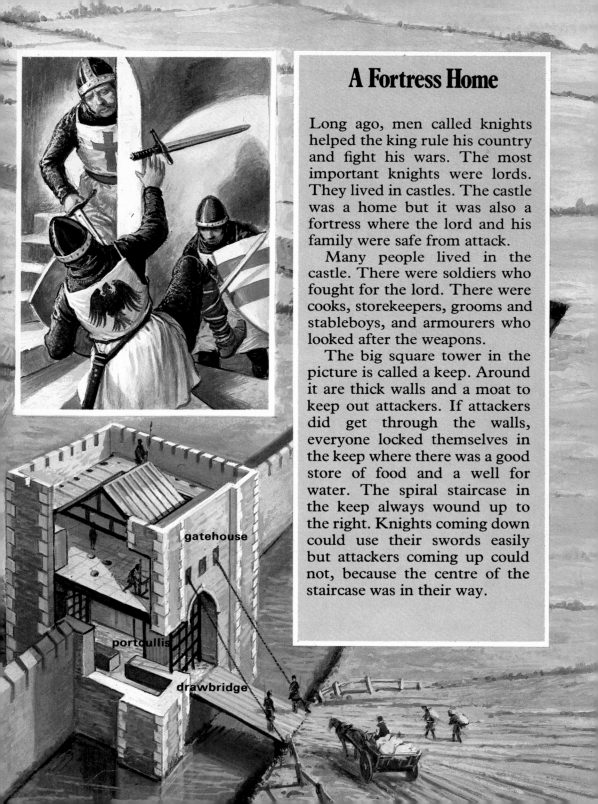

A Fortress Home

Long ago, men called knights helped the king rule his country and fight his wars. The most important knights were lords. They lived in castles. The castle was a home but it was also a fortress where the lord and his family were safe from attack.

Many people lived in the castle. There were soldiers who fought for the lord. There were cooks, storekeepers, grooms and stableboys, and armourers who looked after the weapons.

The big square tower in the picture is called a keep. Around it are thick walls and a moat to keep out attackers. If attackers did get through the walls, everyone locked themselves in the keep where there was a good store of food and a well for water. The spiral staircase in the keep always wound up to the right. Knights coming down could use their swords easily but attackers coming up could not, because the centre of the staircase was in their way.

gatehouse

portcullis

drawbridge

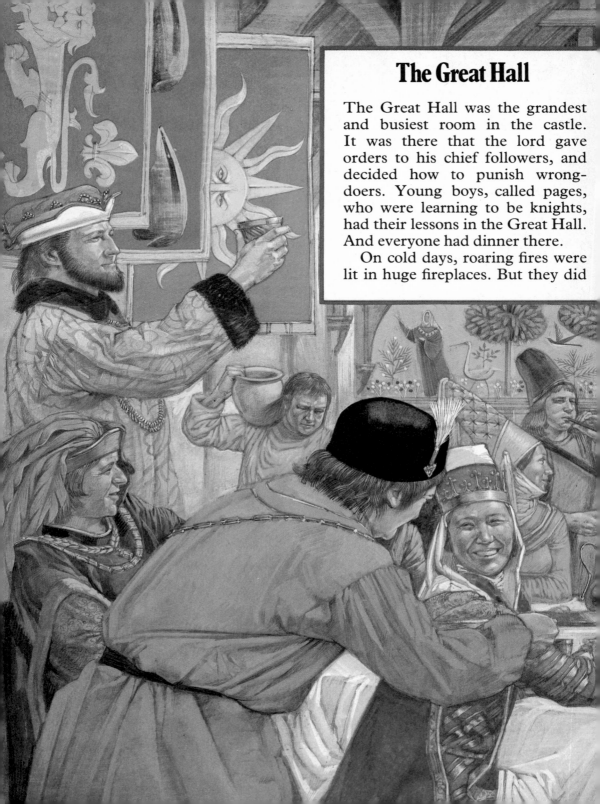

The Great Hall

The Great Hall was the grandest and busiest room in the castle. It was there that the lord gave orders to his chief followers, and decided how to punish wrong-doers. Young boys, called pages, who were learning to be knights, had their lessons in the Great Hall. And everyone had dinner there.

On cold days, roaring fires were lit in huge fireplaces. But they did

not have proper chimneys, and choking smoke blew into the hall. At one end of the hall was a platform where the lord, his lady, and important guests sat on chairs at the 'high table'. Everyone else sat on benches at rough tables. During dinner, minstrels played music and sang songs of love and adventure. At bedtime, the lord and his lady went to their chamber. The others slept on straw on the stone floor.

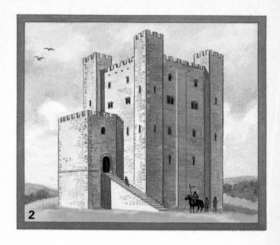

Castles through the Ages

The first castles did not have grand halls or tall keeps. They were simple wooden towers built hurriedly on a mound of earth. A strong fence around the tower and another one lower down kept raiders out. You can see a castle like this in picture 1.

The knights were safe in their wooden tower. But it was not a very comfortable home. The lord and his lady had their own chamber, with only a bed and a chest to keep things in. Everyone else lived, ate and slept in the draughty hall.

Soon the knights began building stronger castles of stone. Like the wooden castles, these had a huge keep with walls around it. You can see the stone keep in picture 2.

Later castles, like the one in picture 3, had even thicker and stronger walls with towers built into them. Each tower was like a little keep. Soldiers on top of the high walls could drop rocks and aim arrows on attackers below. They could also shoot arrows and hurl spears through narrow slits in the towers. Instead of a keep, there was a fine house for the lord and his family inside the walls. There were also kitchens, stables, barns, a chapel, and other buildings. It was rather like a small village.

As time passed, the knights built even more massive castles. Picture 4 shows one perched on top of a rocky hill. It was very hard to attack. Archers defending the castle could fire arrows from the top of the high walls as well as from the low wall around it. Picture 5 shows a fine castle with a moat, a deep ditch filled with water, as well as solid, high walls. The huge gatehouse was as strong as a keep. It was a last refuge for the lord and his followers if attackers succeeded in storming the castle walls.

Armour

Knights wore armour to protect themselves in battle. In Norman times, they wore armour made of tiny metal rings linked together like chains. It was called chain mail. They also wore thick padded vests to soften blows. Chain mail protected knights from cutting blows from an enemy sword. But it did not stop a fast flying arrow, or a thrust from the sharp tip of a sword or spear.

Saracen and Christian knights who fought one another during the Crusades also wore chain mail. But a new kind of armour guarded their knees. It was called plate armour, and was made of thin sheets of iron or steel. This new armour protected knights so well in battle that they were soon wearing complete suits made of metal plate. Metal plates were shaped to fit different parts of their bodies. The plates were hinged or strapped together so the knight could move easily. In his heavy suit of shining armour, a knight could ride unharmed through a shower of arrows. And sword blows simply slipped off the smooth metal. Knights now used iron clubs and maces to topple one another from their horses.

coats-of-arms

14th century helmet

15th century spur

15th century helmet

Knights in battle had to know friend from foe. But their faces were hidden by the visors of their helmets. So each knight had a special picture or pattern of his own. This was his coat-of-arms. It was painted on shields and stitched on tunics, flags and banners. Some of the simple patterns used in coats-of-arms are shown in the picture.

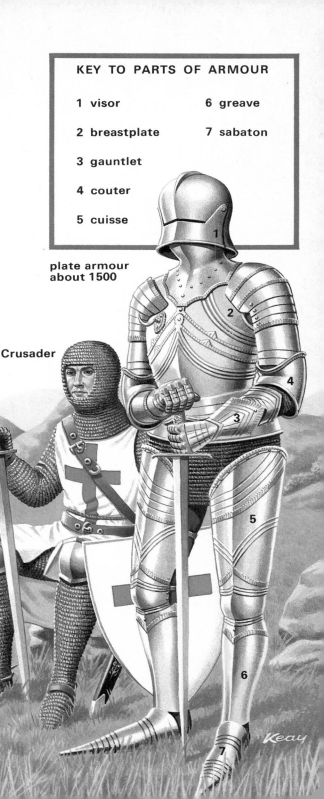

KEY TO PARTS OF ARMOUR

1 visor	6 greave
2 breastplate	7 sabaton
3 gauntlet	
4 couter	
5 cuisse	

plate armour
about 1500

Norman

Saracen

Crusader

3th century helmet

Squire to Knight

In the days of knights and castles, children did not have to go to school. Instead, noblemen sent their sons to live in a castle to learn to be knights.

The boys began their training as pages. They waited on the ladies at dinner. They learned to read, write and count, to sing and to write poems. They were taught how to hunt and how to fight. But most important of all, they learned to be kind, honest, brave and loyal.

When they were fourteen, the boys became squires. Every knight had a squire to help him. The squire looked after the knight's armour and helped him put it on. The knight taught his squire how to fence with a sword and tilt with a lance.

When he was twenty-one years old, the squire's training was finished. It was an exciting and important time. He spent a whole night praying in the chapel. Next morning, the lord and all his knights gathered in the Great Hall. First, they helped the squire into his armour. Then they listened as he promised to serve God, and to be a good and brave knight. The great moment came when he knelt before his lord to be 'dubbed'. Solemnly, the lord touched him on the shoulder with his sword, saying 'I dub thee knight. Arise!'

The Joust

A knight was a soldier and it was his duty to fight for his lord. When knights were not fighting, they could show their skill and bravery in a tournament. This was a friendly but dangerous mock battle. Tournaments were held on holidays or when important visitors came to stay at the castle. There was fun and games for everyone on the day of the tournament. It was rather like a fair. Gaily coloured tents were put up, and people came from miles around to enjoy the noise and excitement.

Squires helped their knights put on full battle armour and mount their brightly robed horses. A fanfare of trumpets sounded and a herald appeared to announce the contest. Most popular and exciting of the mock battles were jousts.

In a joust, two knights on horseback charged at each other with blunted wooden lances. Each tried to unseat his opponent from his horse. The fighting was so fierce that a lance was easily broken. The young squires stood by, each ready to help his knight up if he was toppled from his horse, or to hand him a new lance.

Sometimes there was also a tourney. In a tourney, two bands of knights fought each other with swords. This was good training for a real battle. The knights charged at great speed and fought with such force that they were often badly hurt. At the end of the day, the knights who had fought most bravely were declared the champions.

The Siege

Breaking into a castle was a difficult and dangerous task. Sometimes the attackers dug tunnels under the walls or smashed a hole in the wall with a heavy pole called a battering ram. They used long ladders to scale the high castle walls. And they hurled rocks and blazing arrows from huge catapults. The defenders fired arrows through the gaps in the battlements. And they dropped heavy boulders on the enemy, or poured down boiling oil.

A siege was one of the best ways to weaken a castle's strength. The attackers camped at a safe distance from the castle and stopped anyone taking food and

other supplies to the people inside. After a time, the people in the castle ran out of food. Then they had to give in. But the siege did not always work. Some castles had a secret gate at the back. It was called the salleyport. At night, the castle's soldiers could slip quietly through this secret gate and make a surprise attack on the enemy camp.

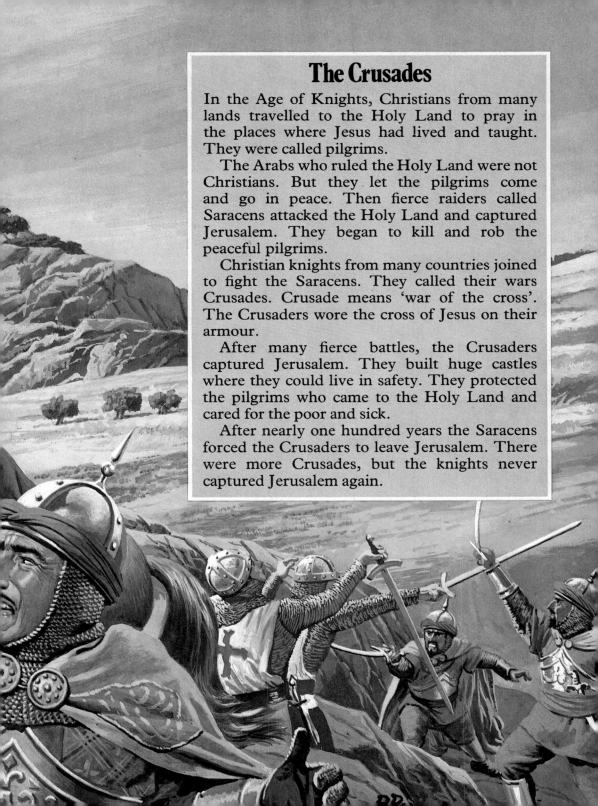

The Crusades

In the Age of Knights, Christians from many lands travelled to the Holy Land to pray in the places where Jesus had lived and taught. They were called pilgrims.

The Arabs who ruled the Holy Land were not Christians. But they let the pilgrims come and go in peace. Then fierce raiders called Saracens attacked the Holy Land and captured Jerusalem. They began to kill and rob the peaceful pilgrims.

Christian knights from many countries joined to fight the Saracens. They called their wars Crusades. Crusade means 'war of the cross'. The Crusaders wore the cross of Jesus on their armour.

After many fierce battles, the Crusaders captured Jerusalem. They built huge castles where they could live in safety. They protected the pilgrims who came to the Holy Land and cared for the poor and sick.

After nearly one hundred years the Saracens forced the Crusaders to leave Jerusalem. There were more Crusades, but the knights never captured Jerusalem again.

Prisoners in Castles

Every castle had a prison. It was usually a damp and gloomy room underground. Today we call these prisons dungeons. In the dungeon there were heavy chains for tying prisoners to the walls and machines for torturing them. Some dungeons were so small that a prisoner could not stand up or lie down. So he had to crouch uncomfortably even when he wanted to sleep.

Near the dungeon there was often a secret room called the oubliette. This means 'a forgetting room'. The only way into it was through a trap-door in the roof. When the lord had a prisoner he wanted to kill secretly, he put him in the oubliette. The poor prisoner was left to die.

Not all prisoners were treated so badly. Special prisoners were well looked after and their prisons were light and roomy. Their friends and families could visit them and they could study and write letters and books.

The king had his own castles where he kept his prisoners. In England, the king's most important prisoners were sent to the Tower of London. It was almost impossible to escape from this fortress.

Many of the king's prisoners were rich and powerful noblemen. Even kings and queens, princes and princesses were taken prisoner. Some were imprisoned for plotting against the king. Others were enemies who had been captured in battle. They were kept prisoner until their families or friends paid a large sum of money to the king. Then they were set free.

1 Bastille, France, 14th century—destroyed 1789.
2 Almeria, Spain, first built in the 8th century.
3 Harlech, Wales, 13th century.
4 Bodiam, England, 14th century.
5 Neuschwanstein, Germany, 1880.
6 Tower of London, England, 11th century.
7 Chillon, Switzerland, 11th century.

Many castles built in the Age of
Knights can still be seen today.
But the powerful cannons and
gunpowder of the 15th century
were able to shatter even the
thickest castle walls. So later
castles were built as fine homes
rather than fortresses.

5

6

7

The Age of Knights

A Pyramid of Landowners

In the Middle Ages most of the land was owned by the king. The barons, or landholders, did not own their estates. They were the king's tenants. In return for their land, they had to provide the king with a number of knights to fight in the king's army

The barons and some of the rich churchmen shared out some of their land among knights. Not all the knights were rich. But they all had to join the king's army in times of war.

The poor people were called serfs or peasants. They worked as labourers on the knight's land. And when they had finished working for their lord, they could farm their own strips of land. A lord could sell his serfs if he sold their land. But if a serf became a free man he could not be sold.

Chivalry

'Chivalry' comes from a French word meaning 'knights on horses'. Knights were the most powerful soldiers of the day. This made them special. But knights were also expected to be 'chivalrous'. This meant being brave, well-mannered, honourable, religious and gentle.

There are many stories about knights riding off on exciting adventures, fighting dragons and rescuing maidens in distress. The tales about King Arthur and his Knights of the Round Table were very popular in the Middle Ages. But in real life knights often behaved rather badly.

Knighthood

Sometimes the king 'dubbed' men knights on the battlefield if they had fought bravely for him. He touched them on the shoulder with his sword. But in times of peace a knight had to go through a long religious ceremony after his years of training. Before he was knighted, a squire spent a night alone praying in a chapel, with his sword and his shield beside him. This was called his vigil.

Some knights belonged to holy groups or 'orders'. Two of the most famous were the Knights Hospitallers and the Knights Templars. Knights of these orders fought bravely during the Crusades.

Modern Knights

People are still knighted in some countries today as a mark of honour and reward for their services to the country. But very few modern knights live in castles like the knights of old.